Journal Of A Lost Boy

Kevin Densmore

Published by Kevin Densmore, 2022.

While every precaution has been taken in the preparation of this book, the publisher assumes no responsibility for errors or omissions, or for damages resulting from the use of the information contained herein.

JOURNAL OF A LOST BOY

First edition. December 25, 2022.

Copyright © 2022 Kevin Densmore.

ISBN: 979-8215600252

Written by Kevin Densmore.

Also by Kevin Densmore

Scary Things Happen in Lakewood
Scary Things Happen in Lakewood
Scary Things Happen in Lakewood 2
Scary Things Happen in Lakewood 3
Scary Things Happen in Lakewood 4

Stories to Inspire and Tales that Terrify
Stories to Inspire and Tales That Terrify.
Stories to Inspire and Tales that Terrify (Volume Two)
Stories to Inspire and Tales That Terrify.(Volume Three)
Stories to Inspire and Tales that Terrify (Volume four)

Standalone
Strange 80's State of Mind
Savage 90's State Of Mind
The Devil's Missing Children
What the Rain Washes Away
Sweet 70's State of Mind
Pesky Little Sleeve Hearts
One Night At The 4/26

Journal Of A Lost Boy

Table of Contents

Author's Introduction: On with the show 1

Here's the End... 2

Break Bread 4

Flow 6

Cold Cup O' Tea 7

Through Shattered Glass 9

Sleepy Time 11

Door 12

Hello Citizen 13

Be My Everything 14

Everyone is = ...16

Hmmm 17

Devil Darling 18

Unlike Today 20

Chalky Tasting Existence 22

Generation Do Nothing: (Precision Division: part one) 24

Big Bad Boomer: (Precision Division: part two) 26

It's our time: (Precision Division: part three) 28

Conquered : (Precision Division: part four) 30

Sweet Angel 33

Cranky Pants 35

These Factory Installed Options Suck 37

Death to HIM 39

Not Everything Makes Sense 41

Old Vs. New 43

Burn Like a Motherfucker 45

For the World 47

Juggle 49

A Letter to My Daughter 50

Pennies 55

La-la la-love 56

Fledgling 57

Chainsaw Dialect 59

Go Death Go 61

After I Found You 63

Gift Card 65

Bang!?! 66

Sincere Salvation 68

It's Okay (It's not Okay) 70

A Letter To God 71

Sunshine 73

Choke 74

Overlove 76

Death Dealing Daddy Issues 77

An End To An End 79

Does This Need A Title? 82

No Power 84

Another Sunday 86

Protect Your Idiot 88

Song 90

I Love, I Hate 92

You Know What 94

My Head 96

Love Thy Neighbor 98

I love my Country 100

Goodbye 102

...Only to Begin 103

To everyone who has joined me on this strange journey, this one is for you. I know it is not a beer, but hey it'll last longer.

Cover designed and Painted By: Athena Fairchild

Author's Introduction: On with the show

Well hello everyone and welcome to my second book of poetry!!!! I want to thank all of you for reading this and for purchasing this great collection of what is essentially my most personal work ever. These poems reflect a side of me that many don't get to see, until now.

There is heartbreak, fear, anger,happiness, and sadness in these pages. But each poem, to me at least, is a work of art that provides a way to cope with a personal matter. Some of you might relate, some of you might get triggered, and some of you might go, "Is he all right, does he need a hug." The answer to that is yes, yes I do need a hug.

Now I will not reveal what inspired each of these wonderful poems but some will have little notes, along with the dates that they were written. So do not expect a special authors notes section at the end of this book. Before you continue I need to thank Athena Fairchild for her beautiful painting that became this book's cover.

And all my extended family and friends past, present, and future. I am not going to spend eighteen pages naming all of you, just know that I love you all and this journey is far from over.

Ok let's go and enjoy this wonderful collection of poems, inside a book with a title that has a cheeky reference to Peter Pan. I hope you guys enjoy your little journey through this journal that fully captures my mind.

Until next time, Toodles!,

Kevin Densmore

Here's the End...

When I feel complicated
I let my hair fall out
Hide behind these walls
That I know nothing about
I try to be a friend
Only to be an enemy
It always seems like
Another mistake to me
What is this lie
You're trying to tell me
What is this bridge
You're trying to sell me
Is this the end?
Is this where I am going?
Pardon me friends
But my nightmares are showing
I try so hard
To try to be better
Follow this game of life
Right down to the letter
I don't wanna be this high
I just want to come down
Because if everyone is smiling
Someone has to frown
I didn't mean to offend

Why am I so frustrating?
I get it I let you down
Because I left you waiting
So let me go down this road
I'll let you be my friend
But please look away from me
And Here's to the end!
August 2022

Break Bread

You can sit at my table and eat when hungry
Regardless of what you believe
Regardless of who you love
Or if you are a different tone than me
Judgment is not my forte
I would rather meet the person beneath the skin
It is not up to me to tell you how to live
Or judge you based on what you think is sin
I will feed you if you need a bite
Your past does not define you
I only care how you are today
I will sit next to you no matter what you do
Life is hard enough
With all the stuff we have to deal with today
I care less about what you have done
As long as there is truth in what you say
So pull up a chair and have something to eat
Let's join hands and rejoice being here
There is no reason for us to fight
There is nothing at my table for you to fear
We can be friends forever or in passing
But for now let us not leave my table hungry
You are more than just a name
And I will never question your right to be
So what do you say, are you hungry, care for a seat, my friend?

May 2022

Flow

I go with it
Then I regret it
I don't know
Does it show
I roll with it
Get rocked with it
Am I in control
Who the hell knows
I pray to it
Then fall to it
What do I hear
Is that my fear
Are they here
That's quite queer
Yet I am alone
For from home
I go with it
I dance with it
I hate it
But I trust it
Here I go.
April 2002

Cold Cup O' Tea

Sitting on the front porch swing
Life swirling like a kaleidoscope around me
Winds in the weeds a whistling
As I find comfort in a cold cup o'tea
World kept on spinning
The sun traveling from east to west
Day and straight into night
Simple days that I enjoy best
Mother in the kitchen
Father nowhere to be found
The dog curled up at my feet
There is no crying or tears around
Everything is peaceful
I can even hear my siblings cheer
There is no one to hold us down
No one to make us cower in fear
At evening we move out of sight
And try to make ourselves scarce
Because if it is a bad day at work
Our monster may be a little fierce
But right now it is lunchtime'
And it is a wonderful time of day
Summer sun and a Cold cup O' tea
To bad it won't stay this way
As the day draws to a close

We all hold our breath
I have even heard mama
Pray for his accidental automotive death
Yet here he is pulling into the drive
Silently we move away, we dare not run
We just slip under our covers ignore her screams
And pray for a quick morning sun
Then we are back on the front porch
As mother conceals another bruise
For now we are not scared little children
Wishing we had a different life to choose
One day it will end
One day summer will be here to stay
Is it too much to ask
For it to be today?
Stay strong dear children
She says through her cracked teeth
Just listen to the june bugs buzz
And enjoy another cold cup o' tea
For Anita
December 2021

Through Shattered Glass

I am broken
I will never be the same
I've been forsaken
The devil even knows my name
I have tried
To find a sunny day
But I am drowning
As I stand in my own way
Good Lord I know I tried
I told a lie or two
I really wanna change
Yet I don't know what to do
Star crossed and a little insane
Broken and knocked on my ass
It pays off being strange
Even though I look at life through shattered glass
I will be praised
Even if it kills me
I will make it
It's all I can be
Watch me climb
I'm getting higher everyday
I will not let
Myself stand in my way
So here I go again

Reading my words out loud
Never knowing it was ok
For me to hold my head up high and be proud
For those that doubt I will stand tall
Above the bad things long past
I will walk away and be counted
Stop looking at life through shattered glass.
May 2001

Sleepy Time

Eyes grow heavy
Motivation gone
I wanna hide away
I wanna be alone
Too many noises
To many sounds
World is overcrowded
Too many people around
Too much stress
Weigh heavy on my head
The world is more relatable
When I am in bed
Good night
Even though it's noon
I need the time away
I will be back soon
One sheep, Two Sheep....zzzzzz
08/11/87

.....I wrote this in middle school and submitted it in a poetry contest. I found it stupid and lazy, but apparently it was published in a book, collecting poems from middle schoolers across the country. I have never seen that book. But my Aunt had a copy of this poem, apparently my mother gave it to her..She sent it to me and now here it is rereleased unto the world. So I guess that technically this poem is the first thing I ever published. How cool is that?.....

Door

I walked out into the world
Scared to death by what I found
There is hell in the world
And blood all over the ground
Teeth have been sharpened
And the devils are in control
I only want to be free
Yet I don't even own my soul
Why is the world so full of hate,
When there's heaven above?
What happened to patience
Understanding, peace and love?
I try to look through the smoke
Caused by our fires of difference
Yet the more I am blinded
The less things make sense
I wish for a better day
I wish that we could be something more
But all I am left with is regret
Regret that I opened that....
March 2022

Hello Citizen

Shhh stay quiet
We have rules for you to obey
They all sound the same
But hear us out, do as we say
Your opinions don't matter
All your Gods have failed
You rockets have no red glare
And tigers have uncatchable tails
Nothing is omnipotent
Except our words of law
Say nothing about us
Or the man you thought you saw
Sure it's all fake
Hope is just as false as you
Do as we say dear sheep
Not as you see us do
This is our world
There is nothing for you here
Just rules to follow
And outlines based on your fear.
We will keep you entertained
Numb so you don't see us in the light
We are your devils and lords
And we are always right.
May 2022

Be My Everything

I have never been in love
Like I am in this moment
You are truly a gift
An angel heaven sent
My heart beats a thousand beats
Just for you
A thousand secret whispers
And every one of them true
You are the love
I have always hoped for
That and a million times over
So much more
I love your face
And the way you speak
Your voice is a drug
And my knees are weak
I am head over moon
Falling all over you
I wish there more hours in the day
Just to show how I am true
I honestly live for you
And I would die without
Your kiss your love
Everything I am all about
I love you my dear

Always and forever
February 1998

Everyone is =

I refuse to hate someone over who they love
I refuse to hate someone over what God they think is above
I refuse to hate someone over the color of their skin
I refuse to hate someone over the merit of their sin
I want to believe that everyone can coexist
I want to believe everyone has a right to resist
I want to believe that everyone will rise above
I want to believe that everyone is capable of love
I wish that we could become a race that is together
I wish that we could be a race where we all know better
I wish that we could be a race that our runs the rats
I wish that we could be a race that is allowed to wear many hats
We can be better
We can be whole
We can be perfect
We can be one
WE JUST HAVE TO TRY!
WE HAVE TO SHUT UP!
WE HAVE TO LISTEN!
I know we can all become one with each other
June 2022

Hmmm

I have a question
Wait I can't ask it, absurd!
Hold on yes it's important
Why do you have handcuffs sir?
Is free speech stolen?
Can I not talk back?
Here we go a collection of beliefs
Weaponized and under attack
Ok I get it
I will survive just fine
But when will I be allowed
To call this life mine?
Hello
It's dark in here
Will I be let out?
Is anybody there?
Well it had to end some way, someday, and this way.
Freedom?
Are you still around?
January 2017

Devil Darling

I will consume you
I will be inside you
I will devour you
You know this to be true
I am your disease
I am your reason to be
I am treason you see
I am everything you want from me
Break Broke Broken
Hell has spoken
Here I am
The blessed goddamned
Little lost starling
It's me. It's me. I am your devil darling.
I will break your back
Give you a heart attack
Big horns and a little nasty
God you know you love me
I will bring you to my hell
A place you know well
Don't ask I'll never tell
Mmm angel I caught you by the tail
Lust and trust
A sin is a must
My beautiful angelic starling

I'm here to save you. Your goddamned devil darling!
I love you too
That and the desire within you
Feast on me, I will feast upon you
Hell is here, yet heaven is what I do
Pray to your devil darling
November 2022

Unlike Today

Today was Hell
Tomorrow may be a bitch
And fuck whatever yesterday was
A cut with no stitch
God help me now
Because I am not what I do
Except whatever you blame me for
Because you said it, so it must be true
I tried
I mean honestly are you not impressed
Or are you happy
When I am beaten, broken, and stressed
Whatever your right
I am obviously wrong
That is such a problem
You knew better all along
I want to better myself
But you keep getting in my way
Yes I heard you
All you do is scream what you say
Stand still just so you pass me by
Leave me be
I am begging you
Take your claws from me
I will try to be a good boy

But I can't be the only way
Why don't you be better tomorrow
Unlike today.
December 1997

Chalky Tasting Existence

How is your day going?
Bad?
We have a pill for that!
Wife left you
Feeling blue
Hitting her
Was all you could do?
Say no more
Look right here
We have the pharmaceuticals
They'll save you, have no fear
Anger issues?
We have a pill for that!
Depressed?
We have a pill for that!
Wet behind the ears?
We have a pill for that!
Mother died?
Well sorry for your loss.
But that grief you feel, guess what?
We have a pill for that!
We use to talk
We use to understand
We used to pray
We use to hold hands

We use to smile
We use to struggle
We used to be okay
With not being okay
Now we medicate
Zombification
We shuffle day today
Billions of dollars yearly
Off of fears
Off of doubts
Becoming victims once more
To a devil with medical clout
Big Pharma be praised
Sheep we have become
A pill to control us
A pill to make us dumb
Slaves to a system
That medicates us into submission
Are you worried?
We got a pill for that!
Are you afraid?
We got a pill for that!
Are you freethinking?
We got a pill for that!
Are you awake?
We got a pill for that!
Are you exceptional?
We got a pill for that!
Time to take your medicine
Join the flock
Can't have you figuring out things on your own
December 2016

Generation Do Nothing: (Precision Division: part one)

You jumped into the streets swinging signs with precision
Calling names and making death threats
Seeing nothing wrong with your position
Tweeting from an Iphone that you'll make a difference
Corporate feeder, you are suckling on the teet
Of all the enemies that you reference
You throw your stones while hiding behind your glass walls
Screaming "fuck the police" with 911 on speed dial
Saying men can wear dresses and women have big balls
Your fractured way of thinking is actually chaotic
You cause more problems than what you solve
College dropout begging for a government bail out
You take your paycheck now, while your future dissolves
Claiming you're part of the left, while blasting the right
But when it is time for protection and safety
You call those in red to come and lead the fight
Cowards with last place trophies and tragically misled
I hate to tell you I told you so
But all that evil shit you fear is all in your head
Everyone has a right to life even if you disagree
I mean you claim that you are the tolerant
Yet you can't seem to stand anyone over the age of thirty-three
It is ok if you want to whine, scream, and shout
But if you guys keep going the way you are going

Pretty soon you won't have anything left to bitch about
October 2022
.....I know this will piss off a lot of people. Being right seems to be a trigger these days...

Big Bad Boomer: (Precision Division: part two)

Stop telling me you told me so
Honestly we all have had enough of you
I mean we tried things your way
So let us take care of you
Step off of your podiums
Put your high horse out to pasture
The children you raised are not idiots
Although some of us are becoming jaded Bastards
Look you had your turn
And your trickle down shit failed
It is ok to admit your mistakes
That ship hasn't really set sail
We are trying our best
But you keep getting in our way
Look we have listen to you for forty years
Now let us have our say
The world has changed
No one wants to leave you behind
We just know that things can be better
And we understand it can take time
We have the ideas
We have the steps we can take
So please no more ninety year old leaders
We need new blood for heaven's sake

We have one shot
But you need to get out of the way
We want to take the torch and lead
We want to bring forth better days
Let us try and make life livable
We need to clean up this place
It's ok because as we work
You will still have your own space
It is time to change
I can't say it any better than that.
November 2022
.....Trying to be a beacon for this generation is hard when someone is standing in your way...

It's our time: (Precision Division: part three)

We are trying, honest to God
But every day there is something new
Something more horrible than the last
And it always seems to come out of the blue
Riots over racism, that isn't there
Trust me we ended it
We brought people together
Because we were tired of the arguing shit
We said ok to gay marriage
Because honestly it doesn't matter
We were the first generation to say
Everyone deserves a happily ever after
We fought for gen z to be heard
And for boomers to hear what is said
But as we tried both sides took it all literal
And everything went over their heads
Fighting for rights that already exists
Millennials you started that ignorance
Because we already lead that fight
And things were moving forward ever since
Sure some boomers protested
But they were far and few between
Yet that didn't stop you youngsters
From making such an over dramatic scene

Look the torch has been passed
Trust us if you watch it'll be fine
I mean honestly all sides need to shut up
Because honestly It's our time.
November 2022
....look this present generation is trying, but we can't move forward when everyone younger and older takes to fighting. Shut up and sit down. Too much noise drowns out progress....

Conquered : (Precision Division: part four)

It happened
It was always the plan
Everyone was so busy fighting
We were unable to make a stand
Left pill blue
Right pill red
No matter what cult you joined
They were planting lies in your head
They lied
The media helped them from the start
If you want to divide the people
You destroy their heart
Take away what unites us
Paint us all in different shades
Make us fight over what doesn't matter
Then usher in the end of days
The sheep ate the wolf
And the wolf was full of shit
Turned our entire world
Into one giant hell pit
Honestly we deserved it
The hints were all there
But we were happy to be conquered
It's not like we were going anywhere

The made us see each other different
Once again classified us by age, sex and race
Then we segregate ourselves
Then called where we went a safe place
It's all over
The world is now on fire
We couldn't see past our cell phones
Or our own twisted desires
The ship is sinking
And the captain left long ago
Surrounded by men in black
Who protect a clown with an ego
This world had a chance
Yet no one even tried
We just turned on our televisions
And believed every lie
It was always the objective
Conquer and Divide
As we fault among ourselves
More of our freedoms just died
They sent you checks in the mail
Congratulations you were bought
Then came an army of fact checkers
Who suddenly policed your every thought
It seems that it is to late, yet it's not
All we need to do is come together
Defy our new world masters
Or be conquered forever
We are better than what we are now...

November 2022

....this is their endgame. We can fight, we just have to learn to get along. Accept that we are all different and just overlook each other's stupidities. Because if we don't we are truly fucked.....

Sweet Angel

Silently I lie
Beside you
Hearing your heart
Beat a lovely tattoo
How I admire
How I cherish
How I love
How I wish
You are a gift
A blessing to me
My true purpose
My reason to believe
Stay how your are
Never change
No matter how odd
No matter how strange
Walk so softly
Hold my hand
Beside you
I shall stand
I love you
I adore you
I will stay humble
I will stay true.
You are protected

No let us go
We have a world of love
We need to show
March 1998

Cranky Pants

Argh!!!
Morning sun invades my eyes
I was asleep on the right side of bed
Now as my feet hit the floor
I see that I crawled out of the wrong side instead
Work is abusing me, taking my soul
And this traffic is a bitch
Who knew that a 9 to 5
Was getting in my way of being rich
Shit at this point I'll take a sugar daddy!
UGGGHH!!!
Here is the afternoon
And nothing out here looks good to eat
It will either give me cancer
Or cause my heart to skip a beat
If my lunch doesn't kill me
Than the commute home surely will
Then into my lonely house of misery
Where my wife ignores me still
I mean does anyone know how to hide a body?
Fuccckkkk!!
Now the kids come home
And lord do they make the house a mess
I take a beer and try to hide in my cave
Yet here she comes delivering more stress

We bicker we whine we complain
Until we are back safe and sound in our bed
Snuggled warm and all is quiet
And finally calm invades our weary heads
Then we wake up and do it all again.
Shit!!!

May 2019

These Factory Installed Options Suck

The more I grow up
The more my belly grows out
I mean is that normal
What the fuck is that about
Everything crackles
Pops, oh hell was that a snap?
I used to run without wincing
Now I can barely walk without needing a nap
Hair was once black
Now its gray and thin
So far from golden
Yet no idea where the days went
In bed by eight
Full day's work by noon
The morning goes by to fast
Night comes way to soon
I get a headache when the sun's too loud
Figure that one out
I forget why I went to the kitchen
Oh what the fuck is that about
I wear a belt for fun
I yell at kids on my lawn
My back hurts just because
My morning starts with coffee and aspirin
The new music is to strange

I swear my generation was greater
Looks like I am another age victim
And nothing seems to be better
But damn am I glad to be alive.
July 2022

Death to HIM

Sorry I don't care
If what I say next wounds
But if I you give me a chance
I'll place you in your tomb
Buried away
Out of sight and mind
Cover my hands in your blood
That would be sublime
I should walk away
Forgive and forget
But if I do that
How would you cry and regret
You foul burden
A pox on your name
White rings around your nostrils
A man worthy of flame
Bastard
You deserve what I wish to do
I know it's not right
But someone should kill you
Like that friend
You know the one you let drown
Cowardly addict
How many have you let down
Yes I researched

I followed your trail
God I can't wait
To see you in hell
I swear I will break you
Tear you apart
Destroy and rip out
That shit you call a heart
You will fall
And I swear I will smile
Your family they're close to me
I'll send them to you after awhile
I hope you look over your shoulder
I hope my presence never lets you be
Because if I'm being honest
You shouldn't be allowed to breathe the same air as me
Actually you shouldn't be allowed air
I'll see you again
As you fail in life once more
I'll be your nuisance and pain
Damn this anger is making me livid
But it'll be all good in the end
Run away little limping bitchboy
Ignore your family once again
I will destroy all you are
Honestly
Die
02/21/2019
....we all have one person we want to watch die...

Not Everything Makes Sense

The world is a landmine
And it is about to explode
So many people standing on it
Yet none of them ready for the load
Everything is not alright
And that is how it should be
We need a few struggles now and then
A hero is only as strong as his adversary
We can all find our way
As long as we work hard for it
Yes there will be pain
But we will be better for it
I get it no one likes losing
We all hate to see a consequence
But honestly life is confusing
Because not everything makes sense
There is no need to give up
We will rise above the storm
We can all be angels
There is no need for self harm
I understand what you're saying
Trust me I have been there before
But as long as you keep pushing forward
You will get what you want and more
So welcome to the dirtball

It gets better day by day
Life is a game
And yes we all have to play
So rise up stand tall
And scream till you're blue in the face
Because everyone has rhyme and reason
And if we look hard enough we'll find our place.
April 2020

Old Vs. New

I have been running this rat race for a pretty long time
And I think I am just starting to figure it out
Yet here you come fresh out of the womb
Telling me about a solution like you know what it's all about
I've got some bad news children
Someone had the same idea way before you did
So sit down and buckle up buttercup
Because the lesson I am about to teach may break your head
You are not the first to think your way is right
Just another failing generation in a long line
New ideas are welcomed as long as they are not forced
So please speak quietly if you want me to consider your piece of mind
You can be angry and call your names
But in the end that never gets anything done
You have to stand in line and run with everyone else
Before you consider the race won
So pipe down and know your place
Before you get more than a timeout
Just because you had the same idea
Doesn't mean you know what life is about
I said it and no I will not take it back
Work as a team or just go back online
Complain, and be a ageist or atheist whatever lie you claim
The world will spin just fine.
Unity is not your way

It is everyones.

April 2021

Burn Like a Motherfucker

Tear me down
Brick by brick
Just to stone me with what I built
God you make me sick
How dare you
Compare yourself to me
I may be blind
But you sure as hell cannot see
I am not your boy
How dare you
You are not entitled to shit
Your mouth is running
I advise you to shut it
I am nice
But I do evil real well
It takes zero seconds
To drag you to my level of hell
I am not your problem
Grow up
Seriously why is it so tough
You lie and you deceive
Yet you're the one who had it rough
Fuck off
Do you hear me
Do I need to play it on repeat

Or will you let me be
I am not your chance at success
Burn like a motherfucker
Who stayed out too late on a Tuesday
You do know
I never needed you anyway
Kindness is not weakness
You fucking tool
I gave you my all
Yet you played me the fool
When I say I hope you die, you should believe it.
I am not your path to success
Sorry I thought you were alright
Mediocre right off the start
You never had your shit together
No wonder you fell apart
Just go away
No one liked you anyway
I will move forward
While you fail day to day
I am so much better without you
Sorry it's true
What you expected me to be nice about your childish behavior.
Don't make me fucking laugh.
This poem right here is my last thought of you
Consider it an Epitaph
08/21/2022

.....Losing selfish, jaded, toxic people is becoming a hobby of mine. I stand by these words. I offer no apologies. Freedom is a wonderful thing....

For the World

Come together
They say
Live together
If you may
Be strong
Unite
No more tears
Do not fight
We are one
One for all
Divided
We will fall
Come alive
Play dead
Hold hands
To get ahead
Shut up
We can agree
More to life
You and me
We are all
We are here
Learn love
Forget fear
Runaway

From the past
True peace
Can last
No more
Left or right
Blue or red
We fight
As one
We win
Then peace
Will begin
It can be
Achieved
If we just
Believe
August 2019

......This simple little poem is literally describing the simple way this world can move past all this stupid arguing we are doing. We are all human. We are all equal. We are all right. Now we just need to be at peace. In order to do that. We need to just open our eyes and breathe......

Juggle

My circus is full of clowns
Who has their make up on to tight
Holding a thousand red dead balloons
And only coming out at night
The lions are running wild
And the elephants are trampling everyone
Yet somehow I find a way
To juggle all the things I need done
The ringmaster is always a little high
And the bearded lady is scary as hell
The high wire act is falling down
And someone just played a tragic game of William Tell
The tent is on fire and the monkey is up a tree
Yet I still manage to live day to day
And juggle all that is important to me
It's ok though people still have their tickets
To the greatest insane show on Earth
A menace in black hair
Cursed to smile since birth
Come on in and join this freakshow
The show is about to begin
Just so you can all laugh
And watch me Juggle sin after sin.
January 1997

A Letter to My Daughter

.....I never told my side of a particularly sad story that took place in my life. A long time ago I was in a failing marriage with only one positive, a beautiful daughter. As me and the mother went for a divorce she harbored horrible feelings for me. I was a bit of a jerk back then but I loved the child so I was attempting to stay in her life. The mother refused. And a lot of drama happened and she managed to forcefully eject me from the child's life. There was fraudulent paperwork, even a threat made against my life. Then they moved. Thirteen years later she reemerged and apparently told the daughter I abandoned her. The daughter reached out and we were getting to know each other. Then the mother once again raised her ugly head and more threats were made. Now the child is an adult. Everyone told me to leave it be, yet the child now blames me for her mental issues, not knowing my side of the story. So many people send me comments this child makes and yet I can't even reach out. Recently the mother has come to me and threatened to tell people I abandoned her child if I did not share with her my profits once I start making more money. That was the last straw. I am done. This is my side of the story. In poetry format. Because if she can be a bitch, I'll be an asshole...

Dear little one, little Bri-Bri

You probably don't remember the nickname

I gave it to you, did you know that

Of course not that family sees truth as insane

Do you remember the first Christmas?

Or the cat you call Raspberry?

I do, and God did I work so hard

For you to have happy memories to carry.
I wanted to stick around
I mean you have no idea how hard I tried
But for every truth I tried to give you
You mother had about twenty lies
Did you know she tried to turn
My own mother and sisters against me
She actually succeeded with one
Not like I needed her honestly
That was cold I know
But I think it is time for some truth
Because your entire life
Your mother just had lie after lie for you
I had a good home
A place just a couple miles away
But your mother couldn't be bothered
She said, I couldn't see you on work days
She let me hold you in a Wal-Mart once
But she was out of cash and needed diapers
I met the guy she cheated on me with
Oh wait, sorry I meant your replacement father
I wasn't allowed near you
Because in their eyes divorce was wrong
But when you're treated like trash
Leaving is the only way to stay strong
I fought, but she forged a test
D.N.A, ask your grandmother, she signed it.
Do they feel guilty about what they said
No because to them I wasn't shit
Your mom tried to choke me once
Yet told everyone I hit her
Yet she never mention how I stood in the way

Of a beating she was going to get from her brother
Good old uncle, did you know
He assaulted her while she was pregnant with you
In another Walmart parking lot.
Sad and strange and totally true.
He wouldn't stand up to me though
Men were too much for him to fight
Oh well let's move on
To when they claimed I left you
Now I am not perfect
But here's a little truth.
I did meet another
I found another way.
I begged to see you
Even asked for just every Saturday
But they waved their papers
Then your grandfather waved a gun
Came right to my front porch
Threatened me, ask anyone.
Wait they won't tell you
But you know how well armed grandpa is
Does that surprise you?
Naw I bet that it doesn't.
Then there I was
Threatened with pain and death
My new life looked on
And stood waited with baited breath
At gunpoint I signed
My right as a father away
I was only 24
Not much older than you are today.
Look I was not perfect

But dammit I tried
I am so sorry
But I had to go hide
I don't expect you to understand
I know I probably could have tried to fight
But the pen was powerful back then
So they took away my rights
My mother had you call me once
Gave me pictures from time to time
Until I just vanished
Hiding my thoughts deep in my mind
Then I reconnected.
And I enjoyed our chat
Then your mother spoke up
And put an end to that
She even threatened your brother
But oh well time to move on
Because you don't need excuses
And honestly you have grown
Into a beautiful woman
And a mother as well
You are going to do big things
This I can tell
I am sorry I wasn't there
Even with these excuses it's not right
I mean I should have died for you
But I just lost the will to fight
So sorry little one
But you turned out great
I am just sorry that this apology
Reached you so late
You are wise beyond your years

And the soul you have is bright
So if these are my last words to you
I just hope I set some things right
I'll listen if you want to reach out
But I can't reach, being slapped away made me gunshy
You don't ever have to get to know me
I understand why
Just have a great life
Stay in the direction you are going
I know you will set this world ablaze
Even if you think your father isn't worth knowing
Ok that's it goodbye and be well
And tell your mother, I will see her in Hell....
10/01/22
.....there that is off my chest. Love it or hate it, but at least the truth is out now...

Pennies

I barely have a dollar to my name
Yet I still find time to step aside
Look at the world from a different perspective
Take my keys and go for a ride
I counted all the thoughts
I sent down into a wishing well
I swear these days friends come and go
Maybe it's the sarcasm or the tales I tell
I try so hard to be a good man
But sometimes the devil tempts me
It's understandable because even with open eyes
I still fail to just stop and see
Life has turned its back on me
And I have no dime to my name
I throw copper to catch a star
And yet nothing has changed
I just want to rise up
See the world from a platformed point of view
Yet I am a failure with a empty hands
Still living life with no purpose or clue
I count my blessings
But I never seem to pass one hand
Yet I never give up and I will always try.
As long as I have legs. I will always stand.
June 2000

La-la la-love

If I were to tell you
I fell in love with you
What would you do
Would you know it's true
I want you here if my life
One day soon as a wife
Forever and always
And maybe a couple of days
Forever in love with you
More than that I will do
A ring and a blessed day
And I do will be all I say
Heaven bound and heart strong
Together we do no wrong
This love is ours everlong
A timeless love song.
February 1990

.....in high school I used to write love poetry or songs or whatever for other kids and they paid me for it. What's even funnier is that some of these kids still have these poems. Here is one of the more cheesy ones....

Fledgling

I refuse to grow up
I refuse to grow down
I cut my teeth
On being clown
So beep beep baby
My soul is torn
I'm a little immature
But life is a disease
And my words are a cure
So listen close
Nothing you do is wrong
Love who you want to
Believe in your God
As long as no one gets hurt do what you wanna do
Oh Lord
We are going faster
Downhill
This will be a disaster
But we will be just fine
If we just stick together
Life is a storm
But hell we have the power to change the weather
I try to be cool
But I figured it out
It's not what you wear

But what your about
So change those clothes
We scar ourselves
With self inflicted indian burns
Yet when we raise our hands
Then we can finally learn
So let go
Its ok to be a little immature
Just as long as you don't fail
Just keep your head held high
As you slowly tip toe across the fires of hell
Hey you
We're in this mess together
Always
It's been like this forever
So don't give up
Because life will be fine
All you have to do
Is break down the walls you built in your mind
And repeat after me.
I am important
I matter
And I will be greater than what was expected of me!
November 2022

Chainsaw Dialect

I honestly tried
Swear to God I did
I minded my "P"s and my "Q"s
Yet no matter what I said
You went after me
With abusive words upside my head
I never wanted this
I wanted to be me
But everything that comes from your mouth
Shakes every branch on my tree
I apologize
You tell me to go to hell
Laugh at my tears
And keep me under your spell
This must be Stocklholm
Cause my Syndrome is lit
Your words are so acidic
Yet I like the way you spit
I swear no matter what I do
You still pretend to be the victim
How can I find a cure
When you're the symptom
Your words cut me to the bone
Rip apart my flesh
And after your done

I am nothing but a mess
Not bloody
But ruined just the same
Why must you constantly
Leave me in pain
I lower my head
So no one sees my stump of a soul
You call me narcissist
Yet you're the one in control
So here we go another trip around
The abusive cycle you set for me
I just pray one day
I can finally be free.
09/22/98
....This was written about my father and never had a title until this year.
It fits...

Go Death Go

Hey hey heretic
Guess what your time is up
The clock strikes twelve
That isn't whiskey in that cup
Welcome the kool aid
The cult like atmosphere is strong child
In a God that someone must trust
We are a pageantry of idiots gone wild
We should not be here
Yet here we are ready for another disgrace
The wounded masses ready for reentry
Into an already violated safe space
Good grief another cancer
Looks like our time is ticking fast
Hey after all we knew
That life wasn't meant to last
You go first
Show me the hardened bloody way
I have some things to tidy up
Before I join you today
But I can almost guarantee
That I will be right behind you
That line is a billion people long
Yet it's something we all go through
I will go out one day

A fragile candle in the rain
I know we cannot fight it
And that we won't be back again
Yet I'll make sure the legacy I leave
Is one that I can be admired for
And when it is my turn
I will lower my head and open the door.
October 2022

After I Found You

Been alone for a lifetime
Broken and torn
Tears on my face
My hearts battleworn
Didn't believe in love
Didn't think it was true
But all that changed
After I found you
I constantly cried
I screamed and wailed
I stared into the abyss
Everyday felt like hell
Thought love was a sham
A game of untruths
But I was lifted up
After I found you
Didn't know how to kiss
Didn't believe in myself
I was all alone
There was no one else
I was so alone
I didn't know what to do
But love became real
After I found you
I discovered love

I learned how to trust
I was able to love
My hate turned to dust
I was now alive
My heart beats true
And it all came to life
After I found you
Love was suddenly right
After I found you
I was no longer alone at night
Life got better After I found you
September 1991

Gift Card

No one loves you you say
Ok , I mean maybe I get it
I mean people still do
But hey who's to argue with a nitwit
Don't be dumb
You're literally killing yourself
And trust me
Your debts will ignore themselves
You make money
Hand over fist
Give it away
To someone that doesn't exist
Claim it's for love
But really it's just desperation
Cause you live in a dining room
Might as well be Hell's basement
Wake up and shut up
Listen to those that try to help you
I mean you could wind up homeless
And then no roses could save you
Just walk back from the edge
You're life isn't that hard
Reach out to those who love you
And put down the Gift card.
10/01/22...if ya know ya know

Bang!?!

It's finally done
The world is on its knees
The skies are getting darker
Hellfire is in the breeze
Storms grow unchecked
The oceans start to rise
Locusts in their little cars
Help the planet die
Smoke and mirrors
We pretend it's ok
But the fact is
We may all end in a day
The devil in his chariot
High into the air
Heaven has closed its gates
While we pray to the be there
The ground cracks
Cities fall to the ground
Pretty soon it will be
Like we were never around
Greed is our penance
Anger is our price
We all thought they were good ideas
So we never thought twice
The plague will soon be over

As we go out in screaming chorus
This planet had a disease
To late did we realize it was us
We had a good run
But looks like this is it
God is ready for another explosion
And frankly he is so tired of our shit.
October 2020

Sincere Salvation

I've been broken.
Beaten down
Torn asunder
Painted a clown
But I managed to find my way to you
I have cried
A thousand rivers
I have failed
To stand and deliver
Yet I still found my way to you
I never believed in love
Until that day
I never fell before
What can I say
I forgot that I did need to try to try and
I swear you are all about
This world I know
You are my one shot at salvation
The only sincere thing I know
I love you please hear me
See me
Oh how this garden can grow
I swear I will stand by you
Never let you go
I tried to run

I tried to flee
I always wondered
Whats wrong with me
But know I honestly know
I am flawless
Because of you
I have become
A beacon of true
Love that is love for you
I swear I am staying here
Hold you tight
Today and next year
I know we have nothing but time
For this love to grow
Now I swear I will never stray
Never walk away
Here we go
All I have is time
Your mine all mine
Now where would you like to go?
Are those bells I hear?
February 1994

It's Okay (It's not Okay)

It's okay to believe
It's not okay to judge
It's okay to worship
It's not okay to hate
It's okay to preach
It's not okay to chastise
It's okay to follow
It's not okay to discriminate
Why must your faith
Be covered in blood
Why do you yell
Protest and berate
Those who just live their lives
If it is a sin
He will sort it out
It's his job
Not yours
It's okay to love
It's not okay to do anything else.
July 2022

A Letter To God

I never said I didn't believe
I just had doubt on your intentions
Suffering for all
Yet you are one of many dimensions
Your resume is weak
This is not what one should do
War, poverty, disease
Yet you still want us to believe in you
Tell us not to lie
Only to kill your only child
Throw down your gauntlet
Then leave us out in the wild
What more can we do?
Limited and varied
Yet it's more than just our cross
That has to be carried
I mean if I am angry
Shouldn't I be allowed to take your name
And do with it what I will
Even if you think it is vain?
We are trying
But you left us to our own hands?
I mean isn't that enough
To get us all to your promised land
Sorry but not sorry

If you want us to hold your name true
Then you have to answer us
When we question you.
April 2020

Sunshine

I could say a thousand things
About what I want for you
All the wishes you had
Oh how I wish they come true
Even if you decided to burn
That bridge that wasn't a divide
Then back inside your castle
You decided to go and hide
Yet your words will still live on
I will not deny your existence
Even if your vanish act
Is weakened by your persistence
You are still a friend
Even if you think less of me
We worked more than just a stitch
Yet you chose prosperity over family
But that's ok I want you
To just stand up and shine
I am sure amends will find a way
It'll just take some time.
....ya know who you are....
August 2022

Choke

Holding me by my throat
Make me struggle as always
Seems like the more I give
The more you want these days
You say forgive me
I literally cannot
You took my heart killed it
And left it to rot
I tried to be better
Yet you brought out the worst in me
I tried to pretend to be blind
But you knew I could see
All the things you did
How dare you cast blame
I never lied to you
Yet you defecated on my name
Look this is what you wanted
Go the fuck away
Leave me be you snake
We will all be happier this way.
Take your fangs from my soul
And your hands from my heart
I think I have had enough
Tearing me apart
Goodbye

Good riddance
Good luck
April 1999

Overlove

You are my angel
My savior of grace
You held me up
Took those tears from my face
Healed my heart
Made me believe
So beside you I stand
I can never leave
This might seem a bit strong
But I am here with you
Staying high
And pure love so true
The light in your eyes
Shine my darkest day
Your faith in me
Helps me on my way
Arms of paradise
And a kiss so strong
Who knew that love
Was out there all along
So my glorious angel
Let's walk into the sun
Let our love warm the world
As two hearts become one
November 2014

Death Dealing Daddy Issues

I did as you said
Even though I saw what you did
I tried to be a good man
Yet you treated me like a kid
Damn you
Yes I rose up
Matured more than most
Yet you called me villain'
Strapped me to the whipping post
Damn you

I tried I mean I really did
Yet all I got was redirection
I looked at you for the cure
All you were was an infection
Fuck you
Yes I am angry
How could I not be
You were to hold me up
Yet all you did was break me
Fuck you
Fuck it
I tried
I will march my on path
I will beat my own drum

I am off your track
Let my motor hum
I hope it hurts you
I hope you realize you failed
I am above you
So go to hell.
February 2020

An End To An End

Uh oh Here we go!
The end is here
It is on our billboards
The signs be everywhere
Can't you see the hungry hordes
Maskless
Faceless
Oh my God we're going to die
Then again maybe not
Holy shit look at that
We all survived
A few hundred thousand gone
But over seven billion still alive
Worst apocalypse ever
The streets were empty
Small businesses died
But gas prices went up
And those with wealth strived
You claimed it was for protection
Looks like it was for control
Yet the sheep still follow
The shepherd in blue and without a soul
I mean I don't care, you're all idiots as far as I am concerned.
Yet here we are
Still standing and proud

Stifled and martyred
Just so you can stay loud
Godless
Fearless
Yet literally have no idea where you're going
Uh oh there you go,
Listen up
I have so much to say
You are a wasted youth
Who piss away their glory days
Idiots who think a screen is a God
Worshiping skinny morons on the Tik Tok
A group of dipshits
Who have no value in their stock
You're about to be abandoned
Reset lets start over again
Who knew the next generation
Would let this world end
Living with mommy
As she goes broke, you grow fat
She is alone and an empty shell
Yet you're irresponsible, how about that
Life is supposed to be hard
It is supposed to suck
You self serving, manipulating
Lazy dumb fuck
This entire generation
Will kill us all
They're trying to
Bringing guns to every public hall.
Prove me wrong.
Oh wait you'll fail

And like always here comes mommy
Cell phone and bail
Why is the "WOKE" Generation responsible for the most mass
shootings?
Murderers
Thieves
Idiots
Ladies and gentlemen I give you GEN Z

I said what I said.
I am just thankful that when it's your turn to rule the world
I'll be dead.
05/29/22

Does This Need A Title?

I try not to fuck up
I do it anyway
Watch me do it
Day by day
Relevance is behind me
I just wanna face forward
Fuck what did I do now
Look I know you're not right
Maybe You're not wrong
Maybe you're weak
Maybe you're strong
Who gives a fuck
Just be you
You can't please everyone
They'll hate you because they can
They'll bad mouth because they can
You did nothing wrong
They're just assholes
Fuck 'em;
Fuck 'em
Fuck 'em
Stand up stay strong
You're not wrong
Believe what you want
You are in the right

Stand tall and fight
Be yourself
You are the only you so take care of you.
Fuck those who:
Judge
Hate
Bully
You are better than all. Believe that!
December 2016

No Power

I am strong
You will not break me
I will rise
You will see
I am the one
To defeat you
You know me
Don't you
I won't fail
I will stand
This is my world
My land
You are wrong
I am right
I am the day
You are night
Monsters be gone
I am alive
I am above
I am alright
I will stay up
Move ahead
Your lies gone
Your jealousy dead
I am strong

You will see

You have no power

Over me.

May 1998

....Sent this to my dad after I walked away from him and his abuse. I am so glad I did. Even happier I found it. Maybe someone will see this and escape their abuser. One can hope....

Another Sunday

No one knows.
Why the preacher lies
A thousand stories
A million false goodbyes
Sister Prays
Brother fights
Father is wrong
Mother is right
Little halos litter the ground
Devil horns rise with pride
Jesus Christ come to life
Just a victim of Filicide
Pray for the prey
Everyone is weak
Now all rise
For a brand new week
Oh my God
Here it is Another Sunday full of rain
But why are the pews
Only filled with fools ready to reign
This has got to stop
No light is shining through
We can't do what you say
Because we've seen what you do.
Please someone save us

Everything is gone insane
We need another savior
Because the one we have loves to see us in pain.
All rise
Sing a song
The message is right
The place is wrong
Unholy keepers
Control our faith
Dollar signs
And Jesus is replaced
Might as well put the devil in charge
It feels that way
For the love of God
Why is it a curse to be a victim of another Sunday
I want to believe
I tried to believe
I wish to believe
I pray to believe
But all of this makes no sense to me
God if you can hear us
Now is the time to let us know
May 2022

Protect Your Idiot

Down here on Earth
Everything has gone to hell.
To many chiefs not enough Indians
Everyone has a lie to tell
No thought process
Their stares all cold and empty
Tik Toking through the weekend
Sheep complaining their not free
Better Protect your Idiot
The world has been known to bite
Little lamb can't control her feelings
Always wrong but says she right
Big brother stalking bathrooms
Claiming his dress is tight
Uncommon whore for the nomads
You should see it, it is such a sight
Dear god where are we going
Why are we all this way
Looks like we're heading nowhere
That;s how things are done these days
We all cast stones
But complain about the waves we make
We are all handed freedom
But some would trade it for cake
No one is right

No one is innocent
You are all dumb as fuck
Protect your idiot
He needs your vote
Protect your idiot
Honestly he is all you have left.
March 2022

Song

You said my name
Called it twice
Gave me your heart
Even though mine is ice
You held me up
Help me see
That falling in love
Is as easy as can be
You told me prayers
Gave me a wish
Made me fall
After only one kiss
And I know
Love can be wrong
Yet here we are
Singing a song
Hoping this love
Will always last
Not like the ones
Left in the past
You made me bright
You make me shine
You helped heal
This heart of mine
So here we go

Around this world
A happy boy
A happy girl
I love you
What more is there to say
Just another song
For this great day!
April 2010

I Love, I Hate

I love who I am
I hate my life
I love where I am going
I hate the strife
I love what I have become
I hate what I do
I love you all
Yet I hate you
I love the rise
I hate the fall
I love the world
I hate you all
I love the world
I hate the earth
I love what I have
I hate the rebirth
I love the direction
I hate the destination
I love the arrival
I hate this sensation
I love my life
I hate who I am
I try
Try
Try

Conflict seems to be all I am.

November 1999

You Know What

Speak to me in riddle and rhymes
Do your best to poison my thoughts
With nothing more than a fragile piece of mind
Call me a liar until you're blue in the face
Cast your stones, break my down my walls
Like opinions really mattered in the first place
You say you know what I am thinking
Yet you'll never think what I know
If life is a race, then buddy
You are moving way to slow
I can shred you with words
And it won't even take that much time
You could never afford
For me to give you a piece of mind
You're such a delusional mess of lies
The more you speak the more I'm frustrated
You're anguish is compared to when a crocodile cries
Fake yet you feel everyone owes you something
Yet at the end of the day you get what you deserve,
A goose egg, nada, to put it bluntly nothing
Sorry if this offended you
But it had to be said
Once you've run your course
No one will miss you when you're dead
Sorry I had to say this

But you brought this out of me
Should have just kept them lips closed
And let the sleeping devil be
I think I will end this now
I have embarrassed you enough
So go walk away and look for other losers
Who might believe you had it rough
Me, I will stand here, head held high
Proud and unmoving
While you tell another lie.
June 2016

My Head

I'm offbeat a little crazy
And all my friends say I'm insane
Oh lord what's going on with my head
My dreams are filled with sugarcane
And bad ideas
Heard a tale that I am sure
Had been told a thousand times
But I am standing in line at church
Wondering if I should pray for my crimes
If it even matters
Holy smoke is that a cow with a halo
Do you get it, it's joke
Ok I apologize maybe that was out of line
It's an illusion of thought clouded in smoke
And here come the horses
I know not what is in my head
But the gamble I take is mine
So here we go stumbling
Like a backwards clock unable to tell time
Good lord
Back to the front
Back to the right
Here I go over the rainbow
Good night
Sorry for all the thoughts of you in my head.

April 2015

Love Thy Neighbor

Using the name of a dead savior
You use hate to fuel your fire
Using words of a broken religion'
As a disguise for misplaced desire
You claim to be His child
Yet act like an enemy with words of war
Picking a side when their should not be any
Not even knowing what you're fighting for
You hate in His name,
Hate when ever you can
Honestly committing sins as you do so
Because Love is what your God demands
You're bitching is embarrassing
You're protest a tad bit absurd
If your going to claim be the mouth of God
At least understand his words
God will not ask you
About the two men married down the street
He will not ask you about the abortion
By a woman you probably will never meet
He will ask you about how you loved them
And if you did so with all your heart
God asks you to love everyone, even if they sin
And some of you failed to do your part.
So please stop causing fights

In the name of of your savior
Do what he says and for once in your lives
Love thy neighbor....

August 2022

I love my Country

I love my country
But I hate the fact that our aspiring leaders fight like children on a playground
I love my country
But I hate the fact that we care more about starving displaced refugees
Than our starving displaced veterans
I love my country
But I hate the fact that people care more about guns than children
I love my country
But I hate the fact that we care more about where someone uses a bathroom,
Than what a person is like on the inside
I love my country
But I hate the fact that more men of God have molested children than transgenders
I love my country
But I hate the fact that the measure of a man's work is not rated by how hard he works
But by the quality if his piss
I love my country
But I hate the fact that more black people are in prison instead of college
I love my country
But I hate the fact that we still segregate ourselves
I love my country

But I hate the fact that more people believe in angels than their fellow
man
I love my country
But I fear my government
I love my country
But the people need some serious help....
May 2017

Goodbye

Goodbye to you
Goodbye my friends
Goodbye to beginnings
Goodbye to the end
Goodbye to love
Goodbye to hate
Goodbye to pain
Goodbye to those who wait
Goodbye cruel world
Goodbye my child
Goodbye to captivity
Goodbye to the wild
Goodbye everyone
Goodbye my pet
Goodbye to those I know
Goodbye to those not yet met
Goodbye, yet I will return
Goodbye I am just taking a break
Goodbye
Goodbye
Goodbye
December 2022

...Only to Begin

One more morning
God what a beautiful day
I will put my head on straight
And get out of my own way
Stand strong on ever shore
Know what I can do
Share my world with others
Who can keep me true
Here we go again
Backing away from hell
Buying back the pieces
Of my heart that I tried to sell
I will grow and grow
Into the tallest one of all
No more bricks and mortar
To add to the useless wall
I know why I walked out
I should have stayed
Yet this world is a game
You'll lose if you never play
My head held high
And I'm about to knock out
This fear and insecurity
That my life was once all about
So welcome back

I will hold the door for you
Impress myself and others
With all the cool things I can do
So no more questions
All my doubts must come to an end
I closed the door and woke up
Said goodbye only to begin
Once again.
August 2022

About the Author

Kevin began writing short stories when he was an awkward teenager living in a small town in Alabama. Now as an awkward adult, Kevin now lives in a small town in Illinois and still writes short stories. Only this time he is releasing his madness into the world.

Read more at https://books2read.com/rl/WYaLOW.